U Are What U Tweet Dot Com

Jennifer "drJ" Thibeaux

DISCLAIMER
This book was written to introduce social media concepts and strategies
Sample scenarios in this book are fictitious. Any similarity to actual persons, living or dead, is coincidental.

www.Thibeaux.org

Paperback ISBN 9798695663624

First Paperback Edition: October 2020

Edited by: Jennifer Thibeaux
Cover Art by: Thibeaux Publishing In-House Staff
Layout by: Thibeaux Publishing In-House Staff
Content Art by: Thibeaux Publishing In-House Staff
Photographs by: Courtesy of The Thibeaux Family

Imprint: Independently published

DEDICATION

This book is dedicated to all those who ever post, like, share, retweet, comment, and showcase the slices of their lives on social media. We're in this together.

CONTENTS

ACKNOWLEDGEMENTS

Before you read *"U Are What U Tweet Dot Com"*, I want to thank my alma mater – Texas A&M University where I earned my Bachelor of Business Administration in Marketing. Understanding how to market a product (even when the product is yourself) has been my north star throughout my career as a leader, consultant, and entrepreneur. I want to acknowledge my family and colleagues for their support and constant encouragement to "lead–win–teach". Words are sometimes all that we have to showcase all that we are. I thank my circle for keeping me accountable as a person and leader.

~~Thank you and Enjoy~~. No, strike that...

SHOCK. THE. WORLD. ✊

--drJ

PREFACE

To tweet, or not to tweet, that is the question.
Whether 'tis nobler in the mind to suffer the slings
and arrows of outrageous social media posts,
Or to take arms against a sea of trolls,
And by opposing, end them.

As poetic as the remix of Romeo and Juliet featuring Twitter sounds, it's much more than words these days. Social media has dominated our personal and business lives. What we see can be traced back to a precocious algorithm and a hearty marketing budget that actually targets users like you. Your clicks, your likes, thumbs down, reposts, etc., all factor into your experiences. In this case, the past fuels your present like never before. There's two sets of groups – those people who just want to have fun on social media, and those people who measure every aspect of your online fun (aka your "footprint") to artificially give birth to customer experiences and improve the probability of transactions.

As fundamentally irrelevant as Twitter may have seemed in the beginning, it has become the "go to" place to find out about political events, get world leader comments, and a myriad of other things. Twitter has become our bite-sized news channel at our fingertips with built in audience commentary. Yes, it's unchecked. Yes, it can be unhinged. Yes, it stays out of issues of tort law (i.e. defamation, libel, etc.) choosing to cite "free speech" as a rationale. There is good, bad, and everything in the middle waiting for us on dashboards and timelines. So why participate? We just can't seem to turn away.

I recall I had a cousin who was apparently afraid of thunderstorms. Just as he and his family moved to a house with a ton of cleared land around them, a storm rolled in. We could see this monster miles away. It was dark. It bent trees. This thing was going to hit us hard. My poor cousin kept watching as it got closer. He was terrified, but also couldn't take his eyes off the storm. He literally stood in the biggest window which gave the widest view – paralyzed by his own astonishment and fear. We watch social media like this at times. We see the darkness and destruction headed our way, but many can't take their eyes off the timelines.

I know, it started out so differently. People literally firing off top of mind thoughts that were typically incongruent with the idea of a "story". I remember thinking how cool social media was because I could get my message out to the market faster in the way I wanted it to be seen/heard. Remember this....

To whom much is given, much is expected.

The basics about marketing have not changed – people need to be able to follow the messages in order to "get it" and "buy it'. It's as simple as that. When the messages are scattered all over the place, so will your audience's opinions and focus. No matter how simple the tool looks to the end users, the most popular tools are literally the high-end vehicles in the fleet. The amount of coding and web development necessary to create, monitor, and maintain a system like Twitter translates to millions of dollars invested. It's not as simple as it looks.

I remember "way back when", I got my first Cadillac Escalade. I was so excited the day it was delivered to my home from the dealer that I didn't even hear "this is what your vehicle's features are" speech. All I wanted to do was drive and enjoy the ride. The problem? Well, none that I realized upfront. I knew how to drive, but I was driving this luxury vehicle like an average car. I missed out on so much the vehicle had to offer. Why? Because I didn't take the time to respect the equipment.

In the case of social media, everyone has been thrown the keys to social media by way of the "create a new account" button. That's it. That's the speech. A few clicks and you're in. Why on earth does social media (and Twitter in particular) even matter?

Social media is like beauty, it's in the eye of the beholder!

The level of importance you give your own social media connects to the audience's level of interest into you and your messages. I said this long ago, with or without you, the messages are clear. Social media has become this personified microscope of our daily lives that people use to understand what you are – and are not doing. It's one of those, you're damned if you do, and sometimes damned if you don't type of relationships. Yes, our status with social media should say, "Complicated!"

The birth of social media has happened. There's no putting the baby back in the womb on this one. We're now out of the toddler years in Twitter, I'd like to think most people in society are social media "tweens". We're at a stage when we may know better, but we fail to consistently do better.

Whether you agree with me or not, the train has left the station on social media. Like it or not, it has become a part of our ecosystem of communication and a barometer for events that impact our lives from elections, to natural disasters, to the economy, to entertainment. What people do, say, and even a showcase through images and videos becomes a permanent part of our ethos that we can no longer disassociate.

Social media is a reflection of us. To be a tween again is to understand that we don't know everything, but we must focus on knowing more for the greater good of our own growth and development.

These days folks use Twitter like a megaphone to broadcast their position on topics and even life. We post, reply, like, retweet, quote retweet, and pin like it's monumental. You read some people's posts like somehow, they believe they've "set the record straight"!

Twitter is entertaining. Twitter is not the game changer many hope it will be. Twitter is the #6 social media platform in the social media food chain.

Yes, NUMBER SIX.

Let's start here, there are just fewer people on

Twitter and that means a smaller audience to hear you. Next social media is visual and most rant with words only. When you post with words only, people gravitate to the pretty pictures on the posts, and stop looking at yours. What can I say, we're tweens right?!?!

Let's face it we're not a reading society.

Most users of Twitter have small intimate audiences that either know them personally or are comprised of people who have never met them. When you go "off the rails" on social media, you're not changing the world. In fact, you only stand to change your own world. That small intimate group following you will either be more attracted or repulsed by your messaging. Either way, it's a small group and you roll the dice with how they perceive you when you post.

When you Tweet, you brand yourself.

I want folks to stop fooling themselves. You cannot brand someone else on social media through your tweets. No matter how good, bad, or even salacious your commentary is about someone else, it just goes nowhere fast. Most people don't have the power to recreate the wheel. And yet they try (and fail) every day.

To work at "bringing someone down" on social media is a complete waste of time for the poster and the readers. Like reality shows, it's entertaining to some, but no real progress is made in life. Aren't we all about moving forward?

BEING A SOCIAL INFLUENCER

Somehow when Twitter gave people the ability to create an account some folks felt they were bestowed the gift of influencing others by the mentions and tags in their posts.

WRONG. WRONG. WRONG.

And it's actually sad reading posts of people who jump on the platform to use it for social fear mongering. I know we have a situation in the States I call Poli-Twitter. That's the ugly marriage of politics and Twitter. I'm not touching that hate with a 10-foot pole. But just because you post something doesn't make it so (about yourself or others).

Becoming an influencer means you have become an authority on a topic or set of ideals. It is not given to you magically. Just like in life, this is earned. While it may seem productive to have thousands of Tweets and Likes, influencing takes time and the right combination of messages. My favorite phrase is...

You are what you tweet dot com!

You are everything your message is. Happy messages reflect you. Sad messages reflect you. Hate-filled messages reflect you. The author becomes the ambassador for the posts.

Before you click on that plus sign ask yourself what message(s) are you adding to the world? You must live with your words. Plan to live it in accordance with your brand, versus the messages branding how you'll live. Something to think about as we begin.

1

THE GREAT MISUNDERSTANDING (ABOUT SOCIAL MEDIA)

Several years ago, I wrote the eBook on Twitter, "UAreWhatUTweet.com" that simply addressed "getting into the game" and how to use it...or not use it. I wanted people to understand the ins and outs of this new form of 140-character communication (now 280 characters). What I got in the process was an education of massive proportions.

MY PROCESS

In 2008, I studied the existing Twitter accounts that were successful and some that were surprisingly not. I wanted to "crack the code" of "Twitter success". Additionally, I began tweeting like crazy! Every little thing about my day I tweeted to understand the impact of the message. Would people re-tweet it; follow me back; reply to me? I wanted to know the impact of the message along with the impact of the timing of the message. There are some people who believe that timing is everything – I believe there is more to it than just timing.

AS THE PROCESS CONTINUED

I realized that my constant tweets (like several in an hour) were all so random that my followers couldn't consistently get on board. You see at the time I had a production company; was hosting a couple of radio shows; was still conducting private research on human performance technology; booking speaking gigs; was a single mom raising an active child; and the list could go on. Accepting the fact that my circumstances were unique, I realized that one person could not relate or be interested in all the facets of my life.

LIGHT BULB MOMENT

I decided to segment my Twitter accounts so that the messages were clear. I created an account for my production pursuits. Therefore, all of my documentary filmmaking projects and messages were placed in that silo. I did the same for all of my other interests that I knew I had enough material to tweet often. When it was all said and done, I had 10 Twitter accounts (I know Twitter would hate to hear that). I went from having one to managing the messages on 10 accounts – talk about an undertaking! I enlisted the help of Social Media Manager *Sendible* which opened a new world of ideas about messaging.

MESSAGING WITH STRATEGY

Having a partner tool like *Sendible* allowed me to give some real thought about messaging, timing, campaigns, etc. The simplicity of saying "Good Morning" consistently became a breeze because I could schedule the messages. If there was a product or event I was promoting, I could develop messages ahead of time (with real thought attached to the messages). This was a game changer. It took some powerful long few days to craft the messages and schedule them… but what's days compared to the year-long messages that were then pre-planned and scheduled? Suddenly I was now free to monitor my social media because the work of the messages was already done.

I BECAME A SOCIAL MEDIA MANAGER

Instead of messages on the fly all of the time, I was able to look at a dashboard of messaging for myself to build a brand in each of my 10 social media accounts. Yes, it took work. Yes, it took focus – but I got so far ahead of the competition because of the strategy and tools I incorporated. I built those accounts to connect with audiences for two main purposes – connect with people I wanted to do business with (B2B); and connect with people who I wanted to sell my product or service (B2C). For me, the endgame had a business focus on all of the accounts.

Now let's get back to the basics – U Are What

U Tweet dot com, right? This implies that you own and live up to the words you message. It also implies that if you are not on Twitter (in particular) your brand is not well developed in a medium that does count for something. Tweets are searchable – meaning internet results can pick up your words. Say the right thing and this is a good thing. Say the wrong thing and you've got your work cut out for you. Say nothing at all and the internet search results will return nothing…and more than likely nothing is not what you want.

BE IN OR OUT

If you step into the Twitter game know what you're getting yourself into. Twitter allows 280 characters per message – and you get to decide the message. Wouldn't it be worth your while to send the right messages? I see people posting a variety of seemingly contradictory topics in the same 24 hours:

- I love cats
- I hate my ex-boyfriend
- Praise my Lord and Savior
- See what I'm doing at work
- Check out my omelet with spinach today

Look familiar? Gosh that's hard for one audience to keep up. With Twitter messages like those, you'll lose audience more than you will gain them. My recommendation – simplify your message, keep it consistent, and leave the grudge matches off Twitter. Using a Social Media manager helps you slow down and think – one of the best secret weapons you can use in Social Media. And if you do in fact want to send mixed messages – tools like Tumblr are more personal and allow for the better expression of messages. It's a blog tool and will give you a chance to explain yourself beyond 280 characters – what most people (who endeavor to rant) want to do in the first place.

THE 411 ON SOCIAL MEDIA

According to a study that was conducted to investigate the impact of social media, the findings indicated that in the last decade there has been a staggering increase in the number of individuals that are using social media in the United States. The number has increased from 7 per cent to a whopping 78 per cent!! That's 244 million people using some form of social media in the United States.

Can you hear me now?

If this is not a wakeup call for you to make use of Social media for your business, then I am not sure what will be.

Okay let's ask ourselves, what is the draw of social media? Why is it important for business? The simple answer to this is because there are so many people spending incredible amounts of time on these social media platforms and this makes them the perfect targets for referrals as well as for driving traffic to your website page.

At this point you may be curious as to how exactly social media may drive traffic. Here is how it happens:

— Social media engages the viewers and at the same time offers them content that is useful, interesting, or relevant to them.

— Social media also allows the users to conduct surveys. For businesses this is a wonderful opportunity to connect with the audience or the customers by asking them questions. This helps the consumers to feel more connected to the company.

— Interacting with the audience allows the company to get feedback on products, policies, campaigns, and all sorts of relevant material. This feedback can then be analyzed and helps the business adjust their marketing strategy where necessary.

— Social media enhances brand recognition. By displaying the product directly on the social media networks, this ensures that the brand is placed in display for a number of potential buyers in the event that they logged on to seek out your services. This will provide them with a further incentive to purchase your product.

— Social media also helps a business to associate with the industry influencers. By making use of social media the business is able to expand its overall professional reach and that of its partners and collaborators. Therefore, the brand is associated with the industry influencer and thus becomes a pivotal or influential source of information as well as advice and dissemination of website content.

— Social media can also be used by businesses to enhance customer retention as well as brand loyalty. There is no argument that social media is one of the most effective feedback tools given that characteristically it is a medium that allows the users to get more social, and get feedback that is sincere and unapologetic from the audience and customers. This allows the business to get more information about the target audience in a direct, linear manner, and at the same time the audience also gets to know the business brand which enhances the overall conversion and loyalty rates.

— Social media proliferation has gotten to a level that it is almost expected by the public that any reputable company should have a Facebook and a Twitter page. This is because this is the most effective and easiest way that the customers can contact the business and have access to reliable information. The implication of this is that the company or the business gets more credibility and the customers trust it more. A business with a social media page looks a tad bit more legitimate and the more popular the brand on social media, the more credibility the business will have.

— Search Engine Optimization (SEO) score. If you are worth your salt in the marketing business, then you have probably heard of Search Engine Optimization. This is basically a means of ensuring that the content of your brand is easily accessible or rather pops up first when one searches inputs various attributes about the brand. With that in mind, every SEO specialist will tell you that social media accounts have a strong implication of the overall SEO score of any business. This will, in turn have an impact on the overall traffic to the site. In a subtle way, social media networks are beginning to resemble generic search engines, ergo it is not possible to effectively carry out Search Engine Optimization without fully factoring in the implication of social media accounts on all the relevant networks.

2

ADDING, SUBSTRACTING, MULTIPLYING & DIVIDING

Math still applies here. IF it doesn't add up, it just doesn't add up.   When social media entered our lives, it was like an open highway of communication where each person felt free to speak their peace. Peace. I'm going to write that once more – PEACE. So much of people's posts are connected to the human desire to he heard. Unfortunately, social media in all of its glory opens the door for the need to be seen – and this need is not always a good and fair human state.

THE ADDITION OF ASSUMPTIONS

As social media was formed, there were basic assumptions about human behavior and usage that became the underpinnings of the programming.

#1 – They all <u>thought people were mature</u> enough to manage their sense of decency and respect.

It makes you wonder why that assumption was even built into the system. Depending on the city and day of the week, we see examples of some of the cruelest human interactions live and in color in our faces. Those are people who are being handed social media profiles with an added layer of the ability to be anonymous! What could go wrong?

#2 – The <u>rules were fast and loose</u>.
Remember, social media was born just as the internet was blossoming and during some of the most litigious times in the United States. Intellectual property and laws that addressed bad human behaviors online just didn't exist.

Legally, courts were asked to fit a square peg in a round hole – and physical laws just didn't ft the crimes committed in the cyber world. Yes, we were learning while experiencing the pain. In order to attract users – remember **users make the social media world go 'round**, social media companies decided to take a hands-off approach to tortious acts, only stepping in for criminal violations.

Just a reminder that tortious acts include things like assault (that's the threatening of immediate and/or imminent bodily harm), negligence, deceit/fraud, defamation, invasion of privacy, etc. It can get pretty heavy quickly in the civil/tort law arena and social media platforms wanted none of that smoke.

What happened to their users who had civil violations committed against them through the platform? They were on their own. Social media platforms wouldn't even provide evidence of the crimes their platform had captured because of their policy not to get involved with non-criminal matters.

#3 – <u>Business needs came first</u>.

Let's talk about the folly in that decision. IF there are very few laws on the books to address bad online behaviors, then the policies themselves were the only boundaries addressing the wrongs. Agree or disagree with it, social media companies elected not to be the cyber police for their platforms. Let's go back to the *"users make the social media world go 'round"* idea. If users felt a social media platform was too restrictive, they would simply find one less restrictive. Ultimately, wherever the crowd went, the dollars followed for a social media platform. Additionally, there's a business limitation to the emerging social media platforms of the early 2000's – they just didn't have the workforce in place to monitor and address bad behaviors en masse.

Business needs and requirements mixed in with end user needs and wants created a dangerous cocktail of an eight-lane highway without lines or police waiting in the wings. What could go wrong?

SUBTRACTING ACCOUNTABILITY

It's hard to believe that social media platforms

could actually watch the activity of bad human behaviors and not take action, because it wasn't advantageous to their business goals. Yet here we are trying to piece together (sometimes brokenness) hosted by the same social media platforms.

The entire system is built on followers and leaders, with the idea that there are more following than leading. This is a reflection of real life – no issues there, except the cyber world comes with an ominous reality – who exactly are the leaders?

Who died and made you king/queen?

Well, to be honest, human interactions died. We subtracted some of the qualifiers for leading when we made it okay not to showcase your real identity. It is the subtraction of light that has invited people from the darkness to play a pivotal role in social media.

MULTIPLYING LIKE GREMLINS
In case you really don't know what a "gremlin" is, I will refer you to the 1984 comedy horror film

aptly titled, "Gremlins". This story centers around the cutest creature called a "mogwai" who transformed from a loveable pet, to a "just add water" multiplication recipe of spawning destructive creatures that wreaked havoc on the very family and community in which they lived.

How on earth does social media come close to a gremlin? Remember the good people – bad people conversation? Enter in a creature in social media land called a "troll". We use the term to describe a harassing person on social media, however the original definition of trolls were bots that were created through Artificial Intelligence (AI) to simulate human interaction and postings but be disseminated for a particular purpose. These bots are essentially online soldiers sent to do a job.

Take the 2016 United States of America Presidential Election. During that time, candidates used Twitter and other platforms to reach their constituents at a faster rate than had been used before. Then candidate Trump often turned to the platform to make announcements, chide his opponents, and communicate with "the world". When this happens, everyone else begins to tune in. With larger audiences, the stage was set for the "just add water" to the gremlins approach.

Twitter showcases what words are trending on the platform. In theory, the algorithm simply picks up on the volume of comments in the same category and displays them back to end users for their viewing pleasure. What happens if those trolls were programmed to post particular words en masse? Now the public is viewing what they believe are "trends" in people's posts, when in fact, it may be a programmed troll (aka "gremlin") being deployed to skew the data and effectively beat the system.

Does the average person understand how trends become trends on Twitter? No! In the early days, Twitter didn't fully understand the cyber-attack happening in their own code. Remember, the foundation was built on good, not on gremlins being destructive.

It has become a "them" versus "us" type of game.

If I wanted to influence a group of 30 people to share and post about my opinion on a matter, it may take a while. First, I would have to find them; then I would need to talk to them and encourage their beliefs to be in line with mine; and finally, I would need to get them to post in the exact way I know would get picked up by the algorithm. How long do you think that may take?

In the "just add water" world of trolls, I could set a program to create 30 new profiles (that all look real with stock photos of real looking people). This creation process would take about 5 minutes. Then I don't need to convince the trolls – they're bots. I just need to program them to post what I want them to post. All of this can take minutes. The Artificial Intelligence (AI) world trumps real world every time. That's just 30 people – now what about 3,000 troll accounts? What could those accounts do? A ton, and we've seen the troll accounts be very sophisticated over the years. They know how to reply to like-minded users who are commenting on a particular topic. They've been programmed to "fit in", and they do it very well. All the while real life human beings begin to fall into the AI world without knowing it. Why? Because we subtracted the boundaries of policies and the law, which opened the gateway for this level of bad behavior.

DIVIDE AND DARKER

It is so easy to get caught up in the web of social media posts that we don't see the division that is happening before our very eyes. Let's put the idea of the bad actors to the side for a moment. Let's assume we're talking to real people (with a pulse – that's the only assumption I'm making about "real" here). It has become common practice for people to run to social media to see what others are saying about a topic. As I write this book, we are days away from another United States General Election where the American people will vote for (among other races) who will be the next President. Debates happen, we turn to social media to temperature check what people are saying. We don't have to wait for our local news or national broadcasts to tell us through their polling or other methodologies, we can see what's trending with our own eyes.

Twitter, through our timelines tells us everything (or so we believe).

Now instead of conversing with the people around you about a topic, you run to Twitter and group yourself up with sometimes a complete and total stranger to talk about the hot topics of the day. It's almost scary that we call this "friending" someone, but in fact no friendship is actually forged, just an online alliance of shared opinions.

What happens when hate groups unite? The darker side of the social media platforms reveal themselves. Again, the social media platform is a communication tool that shows us what people are posting. That's it. That's what it does for the average user. The darker side of the tool is using it to organize for bad behaviors and motives.

THE REAL-LATIONSHIP TABLE TURNS

Alternatively, we see people begin to focus more on their online relationships than their real in-person interactions. Why? Here's what I've found through research:

- You can close the laptop when you're done talking

- You can be anonymous to your group thereby freeing you of the guilt of your words or actions

- You can have an on-demand "friendship" through repeated conversations and shared online experiences.

- Your online group only sees what you show them, versus seeing more of you (hello photo filters)

- And the list literally goes on.

Does this sound healthy? It's quite the opposite. This behavior is an alternate reality and becomes a recipe for depression. As you make more time for your online friends (many who may be trolls, bots, not real people), you minimize the experiences with real people. The fastest route to depression is isolation. While a person may be attracted to social interactions because of the variety and other perks it offers, they are contributing to their own isolation from real human interaction that is necessary for positive mental health.

I recall observing a person who seemed to develop "friendships" with people she had never met. They literally began liking similar posts and even blocking perceived threats. I know what you're thinking, "threats", among "strangers"? Yes, this is the darker side of social media disguising itself as "the light".

You should be worried when a total stranger is willing to share your likes and dislikes of others (who are total strangers to them). The problem is that this twisted relationship feeds a need from the original user – to be heard, be understood, and be among a pack. These are basic wants of the average person. The problem is those desires also make you vulnerable to those gremlins. Yes, they started out like the cute little "mogwai's" but just add water and things can get crazy really quickly.

This is where social media changes from fun to RUN!

No one taught us how to be social media friends. You have people running around trying to forge genuine friendships with online people (who may not even be real). That's worse than catfishing – that's embarrassing to the original user. But people's interest in having a circle overshadows the common sense staring them in the face. Social media has twists and turns, and ultimately, it's up to us to fend for and defend ourselves.

3

SOCIAL MEDIA LIVES IN A GLASS HOUSE

The number one question I ask posters of social media, "are you hiding behind social media?" The sheer question can lead me down many paths; it's simply mind-boggling. Social media – the very place that music artist Drake poignantly stated, "Twitter fingers turn to trigger fingers…". Yes, even Drake can see the writing on the wall for how people use social media.

Yes, real people can get so wrapped up in

what they are seeing on social media that they can become online gangsters handing out threats and disparaging remarks like it's water.

To tweet or subtweet, that is now the question

Social media lends itself to passive aggressiveness from its users of all ages. It gives you an opportunity to develop a layer of anonymity (or so you think) and with that confidence those fingers begin to do the walking.

I cannot tell you how many times I've read a succession of posts from someone – even strangers and felt, "gosh they're mad at somebody". Or I basically figured out their issue and I may not have known who they were or who they were directing their posts about. Scary right? So, what's up with that anonymity? It's a funny thing about that, normally people who want to direct their posts at someone say and do enough to get the person's attention. The reality is they don't want to be anonymous to their target, just to others who may negatively judge them. Truth moment... that's psychologically perverse.

So why don't people just talk to each other? That's a great question! But people have always had difficulty confronting others with issues. If it were easy there would be no need for Crucial Conversations® now would there be? Resolving conflict is hard enough. Adding social media to the layers between you and the other person – that makes the possibility of resolution almost impossible.

Do they really want to resolve issues?

That's a hard one. I've seen people go on and on about the same topic for multiple months, even years. It starts to feel like the person gets energized by the drama they're creating. That's scary to think that one or more people would be interested in keeping the conflict going versus resolution. And yet here we are with case after case reported around the U.S. and world where conflict started on social media (and consequently exploded to something tragic).

Do they believe they're hiding?

I think so. I believe people who seemingly create "beefs" with others using social media as their platform to spread their hate don't fully understand what they're doing. It's like they're "in the grip" (a psychological term) for an extended period of time. Their amygdala has taken over and is not letting go. How is this possible? Those same people can seem so normal at times. But there's something that triggers their erratic behavior – and then tweet-tweet, chirp-chirp – the world sees a new side to that person and their issues.

Blogs are a feeding ground for trolls

The term "troll" seems like such a cruel term but remember, it is a term in technology meant to describe a person who creates an alternate identity in social media for the purpose of posting whatever they choose including lurking on other accounts that may have blocked them. Wow that's a scary thought that people are posting without regard to boundaries and in some cases without a moral compass. Let's also not forget that the seemingly bad behaviors can expand to new people who then begin to respond to the trolls. The original issue is long gone, and people are just yapping at each other. Ever read a blog article and then review the comments section? It is mind-boggling to see the twists and turns responders take - many of which are not even comments related to the original blog post.

It all sounds like a mess; and with social media that mess gets documented on timelines, with dates, time stamps, etc. I've even seen people post highly offensive and negative remarks on their public social media account to only delete it hours or days later. I'm thinking, why did you bother to post it at all? It seems fruitless if you're constantly posting and deleting messages. If you're reading this book, chances are you're an adult. Use your time wisely in the social media space – be productive. Leave the "trigger fingers" to the rappers who battle for your entertainment dollars.

POSTER IN DENIAL

I believe that good people get caught up in posting badly. They start with minor offenses. Somewhere along the way there is an instigator that either provokes or promotes their behavior. Next thing we all know, the "good" person has gone "bad". One of the best exercises I have done with groups is to print out the prior 12 months of their social media posts (including their likes). I then remove the identifying labels (names, pics, etc.) And randomly give each packet to the group. You guessed it, shock and awe ensued as they read what some of their co-workers have posted. Most of the time I get the statement, "this is not real" ..."no one here posts like this." And then the owner of those posts turns red because their "Twitter fingers" are exposed. Keep in mind I'm only printing what is public information which means anyone could have seen the messages.

Many posters are so focused on a topic or target that they forget the whole world is watching too.

SOCIAL MEDIA HEALTH CHECK RECOMMENDATIONS

- ✓ Do review your social media and remove messaging that is inconsistent with your brand – with who you are

- ✓ Do take your accounts private if your

messaging is not "ready for the world"

✓ Do consider removing characteristics about yourself that can self-identify your whereabouts (there are some scary people out there)

✓ Do remove your birthday – identity theft is real and it's still a huge problem

✓ Don't stop posting – just improve your posts one character at a time.

4

PICKING THE RIGHT SOCIAL MEDIA PLATFORM

It is important that one picks out the most appropriate social media channel for your needs; you should make certain that the medium that you have chosen is aligned with your specific goals and ideals. Here is where you can employ the use of the S. M. A. R. T. Strategy to ensure that you create objectives that are specific, measurable, attainable, realistic, and time bound.

You should endeavor to research your key

target market. Get information about the composition of your demographics such as the location, gender, age, religion, income, education level, ethnicity, number of children, and marital status. This information will help you to identify the various personas of your audience and all their probable mediums in as far as social media is concerned.

You can choose to ask a wide array of questions in order to get the information that you require. These should encompass questions such as:

- What are their likes and dislikes?
- What inspires them?
- What is their overall career orientation?
    - (A good example is HubSpot which has done an exemplary job in drawing in these kinds of followers)
- Also ask them: Do they follow the current trends and fashions?
- Are they generally sociable in nature?
    - (Buzzfeed is a platform that excels in attracting followers that are oriented towards trends and are sociable)
- Do they seek out attention?
    - (These are basically those individuals that would perform any tasks for likes)

For further aid in terms of discovering your target audience, you can make good use of tools such as Mentions in Twitter which will help you keep track of the key words that are related to your goals and interests.

It is worth noting that while there is a need for the brand to be recognized as quickly as possible, this does not necessarily mean that your business and/or individual profile should be on all the social media platforms. On the contrary, you should **only focus on the ones that will help you accomplish the goals that you have set for yourself**.

It is also important to note that while setting up a social media page is almost always free, maintaining the page is quite intensive with respect to time management and resource allocation.

For **business to consumer (B2C) models**, you are advised to make use of Facebook, Instagram, and Twitter as they are the most effective for these types of interactions.

Let's use a hypothetical situation. Imagine that

you are the owner of a local bar and restaurant. You then go online and search for a popular hashtag like "beer", the result of this search will be a list of what people within your location are talking about with regard to your services. This will further allow you to interact with the users that are posting about these services and provide them with offers through a simple @ sign. This is an example of "Business to Customer" as in this case you would have interacted directly with the customer or client and provided them with whatever it is that they needed.

When it comes to **Business to Business (B2B)** types of interactions, LinkedIn is one of the best ways to facilitate this among the social media platforms. The manner in which the personnel from *LinkedIn* presents the overall need as well as benefits of social media in as far as Business to Business interaction is concerned is quite interesting. It is important to note that even in this situation where the interaction is business to business, the human element is quite important, in fact it is a core element.

When broken down to their constituent parts

you will find that businesses are groups of people and if you can be successful in attracting the people behind the business then by extension the business will find you interesting. The key point here is to market yourself to be very attractive to the end user.

Instagram has gained a significant deal of popularity in the recent past ever since Facebook acquired them; retailers in particular have given this social media network a warm reception as it provides them with the perfect opportunity to display the products that they have for almost no cost.

SlideShare is another platform that comes highly recommended as it allows you to provide the users with heavy and complex information in a manner that they will comprehend with ease. Often, you will find that people visit SlideShare to consume information that is difficult or complex, to find solutions to specific problems, and of course, to have a sample of some great presentations on display.

Now that we have covered almost all the

different social media platforms that one would make use of in the event that you need to launch your social media page. It is however important that we discuss the associated costs. On the face of it, social media will only require you to invest your time, something like a few hours in a given day, in order to be effective. In comparison, this is a small price to pay when you look at the sales that it would in turn bring if it is successful. However, sometimes time is not the only thing that one should invest. Sometimes one may need to run advertisements on these social media platforms in order to get more traffic to your site, business, or products. Ultimately, your presence is the key element for success.

5

POSTING THE RIGHT CONTENT

Now that you have successfully created a page that is pleasing to the eye and looks professional, the next bit of work is to come up with content that you can publish to your audience. This might come off as a simple endeavor on the face of it but now that you are at this juncture you might be asking yourself, "How does one do that?" Ideally, the first step would be to research on what the competition is posting. The aim is not to mimic but to find out what the audience is being fed with and the reception they are giving to that kind of information. Following which you should strive to do better than the competition!

It may take a number of tries but eventually you will find what is referred to as your tone or voice. Now you can sit down and develop a posting strategy that is geared towards enticing the audience and to spark interaction with them. Do not be bogged down on one thing or try and focus too much on what others are doing. At first you should focus on what works for you or what you are good at. For instance, if Photoshop and Photography are your strong suits then you should start by sharing pictures and images on Instagram and Pinterest.

There are a number of apps that you can make use of that will make your work easier. The following list is just but a number of the content generating tools that you may find handy when they are at your disposal:

- **_Canva_** is a tool that can create beautiful graphics that you may find useful in generating eye-catching and professional imagery

- **Skitch** is a tool that is good when one is working with screen shots

- **Inforgram** is designed to suit all your infographics needs

- **MyBlogU** is a tool that you can use when you want to brainstorm for ideas for your social media content.

Research has shown that of all the content on social media platforms, images and other forms of visual elements such as videos and gifs tend to get a better reception by the audience which is often in the form of clicks, views, retweets and likes. Facebook, Instagram, and Twitter are two of the most popular social media platforms and their photos receive

- ✓ 54% more likes,
- ✓ 103% more comments and
- ✓ 84% more clicks

… as compared to other content that is posted without visual content.

With that information in mind, it is important that you aim to tap into the potential of visual content. Ergo, you should always make sure that you have included images, videos, short texts, hashtags, and emojis wherever you deem appropriate in order to create more interaction. This is a "never leave home without it" type of moment. No one, and I do mean no one wants to be on social media reading all text! Remember TikTok and platforms like it do well because people make time to view photos and videos. Shall I state it again… "the end user makes the social media platform go 'round!"

You can focus on posting images and links; you can retweet, you can post exceptional quotes for your audience. A good tactic to entice your audience would be to ensure that you diligently post the same content for all days of the week except for one where you post different content. The aim of this would be to observe the overall impact that this would have on audience engagement.

Remember in social media, we don't just post, we analyze and improve when we can.

6

TIMING YOUR POSTS

Now that you have figured out the right kind of content for your audience, it is time to consider other parameters such as the time and the frequency of posting. Let us begin with the time element. The best time to post on social media may prove to be a difficult thing to accomplish simply because your given page may have an audience from all over the world and therefore there may not be an exact sweet spot with respect to time for posting across all social media networks. Timing is important because you will often want to post your content at the high traffic times on the Social Media platforms simply because it is at these times that there will be an increased likelihood that your content will be seen by the most number of people; thus translating to better results.

To date, there have been countless studies that have tried to investigate the best times or rather the highest traffic times that would be suitable for posting. However, it is important to note that not all content is the same and not all audiences are the same for each business and therefore the findings of these studies may prove to be altogether not useful. The best way of finding out the optimum traffic times for your content would be through the trial and error method. You can start by making posts at all times of the day through the use of post scheduling tools that are available online and aim to observe the exact times and days that work best for your product or brand.

PRO TIP: Studies that have been conducted on online businesses show that Thursdays and Fridays have an 18% higher likelihood for audience engagement.

What 's the Measure of Success?

Getting the post out is sometimes a feat depending on the obstacles and challenges faced on any given day. But it's not good enough to be satisfied with what you did (i.e. click, post), we must understand how to measure the times for success.

Engagement will certainly be your main dimension when analyzing success. Did users respond via comments? How about those likes? Did they share your post with others in their own circle by retweeting or reposting? I'll give you the secret answers – Retweets are like platinum covered gold bars in the social media world. When a social media user takes your post and shares it with their own circle, that's the equivalent of placing your flyer in front of new people's faces... and it came from someone they trusted!

You will judge not only the actions they took, but how long it took for people to take action. Set some hard stops for evaluation. For instance, once you make a post you may want to consider the following hard stops:

5 mins – understand the impressions (the number of people who scrolled past your post on their timelines, number of likes, retweets, comments, and shares.

30 mins – understand the delta (that's the stats difference between your last time period and this one), plus you generally need to see the number of likes, retweets, comments, and shares exists. You're not only measuring against the prior milestone, but you're also simultaneously evaluating that single moment in time.

Repeat the same checks at the 1-hour mark, 3-hours, and 24-hours. Why such a big gap? You're not the only show in town. Once too much time passes, the algorithm is going to be the only thing that will save you and get your post in front of your circle. Don't depend on the algorithm!

7

THE FREQUENCY OF YOUR POSTS MATTERS!

It is understandable when you would like to post your content as frequently as possible to ensure that the audience as had a good look at what you have to offer. After all, the whole point of the exercise is to ensure that your content is viewed by as many people as possible, right? Well, it appears that there is a limit to how frequently you can post without irritating your general audience and causing them to view you as a spam messenger.

For instance, a study was conducted on the social media platform Twitter and there were a number of users who made complaints that there were some individuals that tend to share their content a tad bit too much which they found to be off putting. It turns out that this complaint was pretty valid after all. Nowadays, users of social media can resort to all sorts of tactics to ensure that their content is viewed. There was this one case that users had installed a plugin that allowed their old content (blogs) to be shared periodically in an interval of exactly one hour. This kind of information overload was definitely too much, and the users began to view it as spam and consequently had a negative attitude towards the bloggers.

Admittedly, this tactic of flooding the timeline with information may have some good results in the short run which is exhibited in the form of clicks, it is not a sustainable strategy and you should definitely avoid it. If your posts border on the extreme in terms of frequency, then the users will develop a habit of ignoring you or will ultimately unfollow you. However, if you are looking to share your content more than once, there are a few ground rules that you can use to ensure that your content does not become inappropriate. The following tips should help you in this endeavor:

— ALWAYS CONSIDER YOUR FOLLOWERS. It is often the case that we can be caught up in the desire to get more clicks that we forget how it is to use social media and content is flooding your timeline. It is often irksome. Therefore, **remember the social feed that you are providing is not meant to be consumed by you but by them.**

— AVOID BECOMING A SPAMMER. There is no need to explain how spam messages are often annoying. Therefore, avoid becoming an annoying spammer by coming up with a schedule that is smart as opposed to one that is largely crowded.

— TAKE INTO ACCOUNT YOUR OWN HABITS. It would prove to be helpful to reflect on your own habits when you are using social media. At what point do you deem something to be a spam? Use this logic to ensure that you do not cross the aforementioned line.

— DO NOT POST ANYTHING THAT YOU WOULDN'T APPRECIATE. Try and put yourself in a neutral position and imagine how you would react if you witnessed someone with an identical strategy as yours. This should be the barometer that you would use to analyze if the strategy you are employing is appropriate or not. This is because there is a high chance that you are not the only one who would feel the same way.

— ALWAYS AIM TO OFFER VALUE. As it was earlier mentioned, there is nothing wrong in posting content more than once provided that you are reposting this content with an aim to provide value to your audience. If the aim is simply to flood the timeline then probably you should consider reducing the frequency of posting.

If you follow these simple tips, you should be in position to develop great social media content that will attract traffic to your site.

8

TAILORING YOUR MESSAGE FOR THE PLATFORM

This is a topic that has been of great discussion in the recent past. There has been a tendency among new marketers where they tend to promote the same content across all the social media networks.

For instance, let us imagine that you came up with a wonderful blog post and that you decided to share it on Facebook, LinkedIn, Twitter, and Tumblr. If you decide that you would post the same message to accompany the said blogpost on all your social networks, then the individuals that would view your content on multiple mediums will just scroll past it.

Why is it important that you come up with a different message across all the different platforms? Let us take the situation that someone has chosen to ignore your content on one platform, then by rewording your content on a different medium you get the chance to grab their attention and entice them to click on your content.

In addition to that, we had mentioned earlier that every platform is unique in terms of the kind of content that flourishes there. Therefore, content will be different in structure and appearance from medium to medium and therefore you need to adapt your content in order for it to fit that particular platform. For instance, there are no visible hashtag trends on LinkedIn and at the same time there is no snippet on Twitter depending on the linked information. It is those nuances that will prove to be the difference in the end.

Keep in mind, that the platforms update, upgrade, and revise their capabilities all of the time. Make a chart with notes on capabilities so that when you attempt to promote a common message across multiple platforms, you'll post in accordance with the platform's capabilities; and therefore, maximize the effectiveness of your own messaging.

9

STRATEGIES THAT INCREASE TRAFFIC

What are the repercussions if you share content more than once? Well to be honest the jury is still out on this one as there are varied ideas as to whether you should post content more than once or not. However, this guide shall give you useful tips on how to work around this. Don't underestimate the power of reposting content as it may help you increase your traffic by almost two-fold. It is a very basic concept and if you execute it in the right manner then it will pay off greatly.

To begin with, every time that you publish a post make sure to include a heading, hashtags, link and share it on all the networks. This is to ensure that this content is

1. Easily traceable,

2. Capable of trending through the hashtags, and

3. Has content that can direct traffic to your site.

However, most marketers will tend to overlook the fact that for each post there are usually very few people that will see it whenever it is posted let alone the target audience. The limiting factor here is their actual presence at the time in which the post has been published.

You must consider, is anyone in the proverbial social media room you're posting in?

With respect to this idea of "is anyone watching" you will have to share content that you deem to be valuable a number of times, sometimes 1 to 2 weeks from the initial date of posting. However, be very careful when you do this. Steer clear from the mistakes of spammers such as sharing your content every hour; if you flood the timeline of other users with your newsfeed, it will cause them to think that you are indeed a spammer and the result is that they will unfollow you. There is no need to force issues and then end up ruining the whole relationship altogether.

Additionally, it would not hurt if you were to add some sense of variety to your posts despite the fact that it is the same content. For instance, you can ask questions or include some pull-up quotes form the actual post. No one, including yourself wants to keep seeing the same post. Most will assume they've already seen it if it pops up again, and you guessed it, they'll keep scrolling. *#MissionNotAccomplished.*

For example, let us imagine that you are posting content on Twitter. It would be beneficial if you were to make sure that each tweet regarding the same content is unique in its own way; you can alternate between publishing the headline of the post and asking questions about it. Admittedly, this simple trick would demand some time to execute it effectively but there is no questioning the fact that it adds a great sense of variety to the final stream. Remember it's all about the finished product.

This is a very efficient way of creating a healthy level of engagement with the target audience without appearing to be a businessperson who is only concerned about promoting their own content. There are a few message types that can be of great help to you when they are needed. The following are simple examples:

— <u>Direct and Easy</u>: Here is where you post a Title and a Link to the content that you are promoting
— <u>The Question</u>: Here is where you ask the audience an engaging question to spark a conversation and keep your content relevant and talked about
— <u>State Facts</u>: Share a fact or two accompanied with some figures in your post to add variety to your content
— <u>Share a Quote</u>: Extract a quote from the

article you have written and convert it into a social message

— <u>Add some intrigue</u>: Publish a message that will tease the audience and grab their attention towards the content that you are publishing.

The beauty of this tactic is that it provides you with an excellent way in which you can try out all your new ideas on your followers. For instance, you may be concerned about various aspects of your strategy such as the efficacy of asking the question in terms of increasing reader engagement.

It is also worth noting that this practice will provide you with an excellent opportunity to create and come up with new headlines from which you can choose which one works best for your content. Social Media and your work to communicate and connect with your audience is in a constant state of improvement.

10

#HASHTAG MAGIC

Hashtags have become the norm for almost all the social media platforms these include Twitter, Facebook, Instagram, and many others. The benefit of using hashtags is that they provide you with an avenue to conduct research on what other users are commenting or discussing with relation to your brand or products. This is often very valuable information that can be used to restructure your campaign. Hashtags can also be used to ensure that your content is easily accessible or can be located by the interested parties. It is pretty simple technique that would only require you to include all the hashtags that are relevant and have a relatively high rank in terms of traffic in your online posts. However, remember that there is also a limit to how many hashtags that you can use without making it confusing and unappealing.

What's a Relevant and Trending Hashtag?

It changes daily, by the hour, and sometimes by the minute. Hashtags are merely ways to organize and categorize messages. Every social media platform displays "what's hot and what's not" in their own unique way.

— Twitter's trending hashtags will popup if you type the "#" and start typing letters that are consistent with what's currently trending.

— With Twitter you can also go to the search area of the platform and immediately see what's trending.

— Instagram will show you what's trending while you're drafting the hashtag similar to Twitter, however there is no easy page that displays the trending hashtags of the moment.

— Facebook and LinkedIn allow you to use hashtags, however their use is far less sophisticated in helping the end user connect with other posts and topics.

IF you've followed my work, I published a "hashtag" series of books. I'll tell the secret here – the title was designed to be a built-in hashtag to give me the perpetual assist in the area of book marketing while mentioning it in social media platforms! ALSO, if books are listed in alphabetical order, numbers and symbols rise to the top like cream. How's that for some creative labeling!

The long and short of it, there are mechanics to your choices if you expect to win at building your social media presence, connect with customers, and jump in the front of the line through creative marketing techniques. Literally hashtags are like the "Flat Stanleys" helping your posts go around the world and cross some of the most interesting people, ideals, and businesses.

11

GETTING THE RIGHT LOOK MEANS EVERYTHING

Let's dig deep into this topic. As discussed in earlier chapters, research has shown that social media content that contains some form of visual component have a higher likelihood of getting an increased sense of engagement as compared to posts that do not have a visual component. This goes to show that you stand a better chance of attracting more traffic to your social media page if you have more visual content.

You can catch more flies with honey.

If you are serious about embarking on a content marketing campaign, then you need to be aware of what will stimulate engagement and ultimately growth. There is no argument that content based on text is forever going to be an integral component of marketing, however, in order to completely set yourself apart from the competitors in the digital era then the visual component must be a key element in all your endeavors.

If you take into account that over

— 65% of individuals are categorized as visual learners,

— 90% of all the information that comes to the brain is visual, and

— presentations that have some sense of visual aid have a 43% chance of being more persuasive,

then it makes total sense to make use of content that your users will have an innate sense of resonance. Next up, here's some of the types of visual content that you can make use of in your marketing to increase traffic.

IMAGES

It has been shown that whenever you separate a body of text with some images that are compelling, there is a higher inclination of people to finish up what you have written on condition that the images that you have used are high quality and are relevant to the content. Marketers have observed that articles with images receive 94% more traffic than those that do not have images. As a consequence of the influx of digital content and the accessibility of the internet with the use of mobile phones, attention spans have never been shorter, which makes content that is presented in large block a tad bit too off putting.

I highly recommend you make use of images that are original or rather images that you took by yourself because this tends to add a sense of personal touch to your content. However, high quality images tend to be expensive to buy or time consuming to create. This is not a cause for alarm as there are resources such as Canva that can allow you to create captivating and unique images at an affordable subscription price. Also, at your disposal is a bountiful resource of photo-sharing sites such as Flickr where you can acquire images for free. However, always ensure that you have sought the proper authority and permissions to use the images.

VIDEOS

Videos are particularly useful when it comes to presenting problems that are common and then showcasing the solutions that your product has to offer. There are often cheaper alternatives for visual content that are available, a carefully thought out video can bolster up your marketing campaign by showing that you are willing to work the extra mile to offer more quality. There was a study that observed by adding a video to one's landing page, it enhanced conversations by a whopping 86%.

There are many kinds of videos that have the potential to enhance your business ranging from how-to videos, demonstrations, explainer videos, and testimonials. Regardless of your preference, it is vital to ensure that the video format you choose is congruent with the personality and ethos of your brand. You'd be surprised how much time goes into a 30 second to 1-minute video. It's normal and expected. Quality and creativity take time!

INFOGRAPHICS

If you need to condense all your complex data and statistics into a visual display that is compelling and easy on the eye, then infographics are your best bet. Additionally, you can accompany infographics with promotional tools such as networking with the key influencers, optimizing your landing page and so on. In this way, infographics can become an integral part of your marketing campaign.

In order to get the most out of infographics, it is pivotal that the design and layout is made to maximize impact. The design must have a combination of all the bright colors, shapes, and fonts in order to convey the data. The information that you select for the infographic must always be truthful, accurate and relevant. Sometimes even the most mundane data can get a fresh lease on life when they are conveyed using visualizations. However, it is important to note that your visual elements need to have some sense of narrative. It would be senseless to disrupt your narrative just to show your Adobe illustrator or MS Word skills.

It has been noted that bloggers tend to be attracted to a good infographic, therefore if you can promote your infographic in an effective manner there is a likelihood that it will be circulated in the social media platforms thereby increasing the overall traffic to your website. The more shares that it gets, the more publicity your brand receives. It is also important that you make a habit of including thumbnail images in addition to a hyperlink to your site in the social media. This will allow you to bypass all the size restrictions that may be imposed on the social media platforms.

MEMES

Memes can be described as images that have humorous captions inscribed. When memes started out, it was not perceived by many that they would have a pivotal role in content marketing as they were only meant to serve as an entertainment tool.

Fast-forward to today's standards, and there's a Meme and a GIF for everything. We use it to punctuate our emotions and create a connection with the audience of being on the same page, and "getting it".

Making your own memes is a superb way of evoking emotions that are positive and also setting yourself apart from the competitors. To begin with, you must try to find out whether niches are suitable for your niche and whether they will get some sense of engagement or not. If your brand is appreciated mostly by young people, then there is a likelihood that memes would be appropriate. Match the solution with your audience (always).

SCREENSHOTS

A screenshot will allow you to provide your audience with a highlight of the internal workings of your service or product. It allows you to show them the functions that you can offer from a perspective that is direct and personal. You can also add a marketing copy and a testimonial or two in order to enhance your overall credibility.

Screenshots are often a great tool to corroborate claims that you are indeed providing the service that you make in your sales pitch. For instance, if your business is making an app and you have marketed the various functions that it performs, then a screenshot with a caption can be an excellent visual verification that your audience would need in order to have some sense of trust in your claims.

Despite the fact that screenshots appear to be the least captivating visual content that we have discussed, they can be extremely beneficial when used as a trust building tool. It would be beneficial if you were to view them as a tool to capture the customer feedback or their testimonials.

12

INTRO TO TWITTER

Twitter in a nutshell began as a simple social networking website that let you share with your friends to let them know what you're doing – right now! Hence the old catch phrase on the Twitter sign-up page – "what are you doing?" Think of Facebook, instant messaging and SMS all rolled into one simple package, and you've got Twitter.

Twitter works around a timeline which is displayed on a single page that's updated every second of every minute of every hour....

you get my point. It's a constantly updated stream of news from people all around the world. As a member, you can add your own little message to the timeline up to 280 characters long to it known as a "tweet".

But that doesn't mean you're going to be able to see every Twitter user's tweets. You can choose who you want to "follow", and others can choose to follow you. And it's these followers who you can converse (tweet) with.

You might be thinking "wow, big deal" but there is massive potential in this mini social networking site to meet other like-minded people, share information and web site links. And those factors mixed with the ability to grow your followers make it a perfect platform for business.

You can also use Twitter to....

- — send direct messages to users instead of broadcasting to everyone,
- — mobile options to send and receive tweets via SMS and email from your cellphone,

— search options allowing you to find Twitter users posting about a certain topic,

— an API that allows 3rd party developers to develop some great applications.

TWITTER TACTICS THAT WILL WORK FOR YOU

For some, Twitter seems like some mysterious creature that's not really understood. Non-tweeters or those new to tweeting find themselves puzzled by the real purpose of Twitter. The savvy tweeter understands the power of Twitter

— in building clients,

— building brand name recognition, and

— positioning yourself and your business.

TWITTER TACTIC #1

<u>Follow those who follow you!</u>

If there is a tactic that is used more than others, this would be it. It's really quite simple – if someone follows you, then you follow them. If you follow all those who follow you on Twitter, you will soon become a power tweeter. Just look at people like Darren Rowse (@problogger), Chris Brogan (@chrisbrogan), and Chris Guillebeau (@chrisguillebeau) – they certainly do this, and it has worked for them. These guys became popular because they recognized the power of the tweet. Of course, you do need a little discretion. Not everyone deserves a follow-back if you feel your privacy and security may be compromised.

TWITTER TACTIC #2

<u>Be a little picky!</u>

Now after telling you to follow everyone following you comes the "but." There will be people who follow you that have nothing to really offer you. Translated this means follow only those who either have information or are entertaining. Follow those who can help you build a relationship with your followers.

TWITTER TACTIC #3

<u>Set up lists</u>

The more people you follow, the more information that's going to come past you on a daily basis. Just think about it – if you are following 10,000 people you can't possibly read everything posted. In fact, if you are following only a 1,000 people you still couldn't read everything they posted. By creating lists, you can easily ignore as many posts as you want, and your followers won't even know you have done it.

TWITTER TACTIC #4

<u>Offer real value</u>

There's nothing more annoying than people who post just for the sake of posting. Instead tell a story, share a news story, motivate, bring a smile to someone's face, and share a tip... whatever you post, what's important is that it **brings value** because when you provide value, your followers will subscribe to your RSS, email, and blog.

13

TWITTER TACTICS TO BENEFIT YOUR BUSINESS

Many people come to Twitter in hopes of improving their business and bringing more traffic to their website. Twitter is a tool – this is what it's for – to be used! Let's look at some Twitter tactics that can benefit your business.

1. Display your Twitter profile on your website(s) and blog(s) with a Twitter button. Add it to your email signature, and any other communications you have. The more you promote your

Twitter profile, the more relevant people will follow you and the stronger your client base becomes. It's also a great way to quickly update all your clients.

2. Track your leads by creating a private leads profile. Then let your sales team have access to this information and make sure they are notified when a new lead comes in.

3. Take advantage of private, centralized brainstorming techniques that can be employed through Twitter streams. You can create a new project where employees can exchange thoughts and ideas. It's quick and easy!

4. You can easily do custom research on Twitter to get thoughts on new product or service offerings. Find out which products and/or services are popular. In no time you can have powerful useful data for your company.

5. A lot of time gets wasted trying to deal with email. The average small business manager spends upwards of 4 hours a day addressing email. It's no shock that

hundreds of emails are received on any given day. You can use Twitter to send and receive short email messages. Twitter has a limit of 280-character emails, but you can say a lot in that space.

6. You can use Twitter to promote seminars, webinars, and new product education. It's a tool that is not always leveraged to its full capability.

7. Use Twitter to centralize your business information. You can create a private Twitter profile where you can upload monthly goals, website traffic data, the latest sales figures, and information for managers and staff. It's as convenient as having a computer at your side.

Twitter is a powerful marketing tool that is underutilized by most small businesses. Twitter's power is in building solid and targeted traffic to your website.

14

MY TOP 25 TWITTER TOOLS TO FIND FOLLOWERS AND MANAGE THEM

Twitter – there's more to it than just signing up and posting. Twitter is considered a mini blog. That means your goal is to find people to follow you, and then to direct them to your website. Here are some of my favorite Twitter tools to be a Twitter Rockstar and an even better business marketer:

1. **My Top Tweet**: Your Top 10 list of tweets

— Find anyone's Top 10 tweets, sorted, and ordered by engagement.

2. **Audiense**: Analytics, optimization, and more

   — A nearly all-in-one platform for all things Twitter. The free plan comes with analytics, best time to tweet, follow/unfollow tools, and community segmentation.

3. **Twitonomy**: Detailed analytics on users and tweet

   — A dashboard of analytics for whichever Twitter user you choose (even yours). Analyzes profiles, tweets, engagement, and more.

4. **SumAll**: Email reports for Twitter stats

   — Sync your Twitter to SumAll, and start seeing daily or weekly emails on how your followers are growing, your mentions, and your engagement.

5. **SocialRank**: Follower analysis to find your most awesome followers

   — Receive a sorted list of your best followers, most influential followers, and most engaged followers. Useful to track the important people to engage with on Twitter.

6. **Klear**: Social media analytics & a Twitter resume
   — Plug in your Twitter account to see a snapshot of who you follow, which demographics you fit, who's in your close network, and more.

7. **Bluenod**: Community visualization
   — Type in a user or hashtag and see a detailed map or visualization about the community around the user or the people using the hashtag.

8. **Twitter account home**: This is the official overview of your Twitter profile
   — Head to analytics.Twitter.com for a detailed overview of all your activity in the past 28 days, including your top tweets, top mentions, and top followers.

9. **Social Bearing**: Powerful search for tweets and profiles
   — Search Twitter keywords, locations, usernames, interests, or followers, then use your new-found knowledge to analyze your fellow tweeps or find new ones to follow.

10. **Stats for Twitter**: A beautiful and user-friendly iOS app to analyze yours and

others' Twitter accounts.

11. **Beatstrap**: team liveblogging
    — Cover live news, sports, and events through Twitter, via hashtags, and collaborate with your team on the coverage. Completed "beats" come with an embed code.

12. **Tweetchat**: Twitter chat management
    — Log in to follow a specific hashtag, hang out in a room that collects the hashtagged tweets for you, and reply as you like (with the hashtag added automatically to your tweet).

13. **Chat salad**: a calendar of Twitter chats
    — See upcoming Twitter chats and when they're scheduled, as well as the hashtags they use (so you can follow along).

14. **Twubs**: Twitter chat homepages
    — Register a hashtag for your chat and collect/view the tweets from one location.

15. **Nurph**: chat planning and organizing
    — Nurph channels let you plan and organize your chat, complete with follow-up stats and replays.

16. **Twchat**: real-time chat rooms for Twitter

chats

17. **Nuzzel**: discover what your friends are reading

    — Find out what's trending among the people you follow. Translation: content discovery rocks.

18. **Buzzsumo**: Find influencers, topic-by-topic

    — Type in a keyword to see which voices get the most shares on Twitter. Find influencers, sniff out headline ideas, and learn what works on Twitter and who's working it.

19. **Similarweb**: what your followers are interested in

    — See the content that your followers recommend plus the topics they most enjoy. View it all via the dashboard or from a daily email digest.

20. **Twipho**: searchable Twitter feed of photos

    — Search by keyword or by location to find photos shared on Twitter.

21. **Digg deeper**: the best stories from your friends

    — An algorithmic display of the top

articles and links that your Twitter followers have shared. Pair with news.me: a daily email newsletter of what your friends share on Twitter.

22. **Twurly**: daily email of top Twitter links

— An easy way to stay on top of the best links in your timeline. Twurly analyzes the popularity and page authority of the links so you only see the best.

23. **Filta**: bio search all your followers

— Curious which of your followers are into football? Use filta to search the bios of all your followers for any keyword you want.

24. **Hash**: top stories on Twitter

— A visual look at the leading stories and hashtags on Twitter. Available on the web and as an iOS app.

25. **Crowdfire**: A powerful social media follower management tool.

— Prune your list of those you follow by seeing who follows you back, who's recently unfollowed you, and who's inactive, plus build a whitelist of accounts you'd always like to follow no matter what.

15

How to build a strong brand on Twitter

Twitter is a powerful tool to build your company's reputation and create strong brand loyalty. Knowing how to build that loyalty is one of the best kept secrets.

Account Set Up. When setting up your Twitter account you should try to establish a username consistent with your company name or company brand. It makes it much easier to build that brand loyalty or company loyalty.

Following the Right Way. Don't be the Twitter person who follows tens of thousands of people and then tweets every couple of minutes. That won't build branding, but it will build annoyance. Do follow those that have an interest in your company as well as those who have an influence in your industry, because you can actually learn things from them.

Showcase Your Expertise. Don't be afraid to share industry news. If you're "in the know," share this information with your Twitter followers. You might just give a blogger the lead they need. Sometimes they'll credit you, other times they won't, but you'll build a strong following when you have valuable industry news.

Reputation & Chatter Matters. Keep an eye on your Twitter reputation. Monitor for personal, brand, and company mentions to give you a jump on any reputation troubles to quickly address anything that needs to be addressed. You can also learn all the positive things people are saying about you, your product, or your company.

Crowd Posting at Events. One area where Twitter really stands out, is when it is used at conferences by those attending. You might arrive at the conference with no one knowing who you are, but by the time it's all over you have the opportunity to have made a name for yourself. The next time you attend a conference check for the official Twitter accounts. It will allow you to stay up to date with conference updates, find out about all the "hush hush" ongoings, learn where everyone is going for drinks that evening, and it's an excellent networking tool.

Building a strong brand and company loyalty is key to growing any business. Knowing how to use Twitter in that quest puts you miles ahead of the competition.

16

THE INCREDIBLE 5

FIVE TWITTER TIPS THAT JUST WORK

Twitter is considered a micro-blog, because users are limited to a post of 280 characters to those that follow them. It's a way of connecting and its popularity has grown in leaps and bounds in a short period of time. Perhaps its ease of use is somewhat responsible for that popularity. Tweeters tweet for business and personal use, making new friends, and finding new clients. These 5 Twitter tips are some of the best out there – try them – you'll like the results.

1. **Choose a username that's memorable** – this is especially true for business where you are in effect branding through mini blog posts. For example, let's say your company is a news company called "CBA News", and the focus is on breaking news. Choosing @CBAonTV as a username would be far less memorable than choosing @BreakingNewsCBA as your username. Put some thought into this. You also want to have the same username across all social media platforms.

2. **Design a custom background** – spend a little time creating your own custom Twitter Header. The ones provided by Twitter are few and very generic. They certainly aren't memorable. That's said do not turn your Twitter Header into an advertising bulletin board because that will turn people off and reduce your followers. You can use a tool previously mentioned like Canva to find a happy medium between customized background, and commercial billboard. Remember the goal is to showcase imagery that builds relationships with

your customers and followers. If you stay true to that goal, you will find the perfect Twitter Header.

3. **Be informative** – tell people about the goals of your business, let them know about your personal and/or professional interests, spread knowledge, and offer support to customers. Don't just post to post. Time is money and those people following you don't want their time wasted. Pinning posts at the top of your timeline is a great way to emphasize a message no matter what else you post. The jury is out on how frequently you should Pin messages. I've seen people Pin old messages, and it makes the account look old and dated. Remember, people who peruse your profile and timeline are there looking for fresh content. Consider at least reposting the content that you Pin so that it has a more current date stamp.

4. **Upload your photo** – you can upload your picture to your profile. Others love to see who they are talking to. It makes the entire experience of using Twitter

more personal. People feel more connected when they can see who you are.

The profile picture is your opportunity to distinguish yourself from the trolls. The more mysterious your profile picture, the more likely you will cast doubt and sow distrust among your followers. Putting your back to the image, a total black image, or even an image that in no way connects the audience to your real identity or brand will set you back in the relationship building department. IF you're in the game of building relationships, you must be honest about who you or your company brand is.

5. **Promote your Twitter name** – add your Twitter name to your business cards, websites, blogs, and email signature. The more people you tell, the more people that are likely to follow you.

Twitter can be a powerful business tool. For many it remains a bit of a mystery and isn't really understood. Twitter is a tool that you shouldn't be without. There's plenty of great information on the web to help you understand the value of Twitter. Incorporate these 5 tips and you won't be disappointed.

17

ASKED AND ANSWERED

TOP 10 QUESTIONS NEW TWITTER USERS ASK

Twitter is a great social media experience, but it can be a bit overwhelming for the new user, which is why you will want to learn these top Twitter secrets.

1. **How many people can I follow on Twitter?**

   A. You can follow up to 2,000 people with no restrictions. Then after you are allowed to follow 10% above the number of people, you have following you. Twitter rules allow for a maximum of 1,000 follows a day.

2. **What are hashtags?**

   A. Hashtags assist you in finding content on Twitter. Use hashtags to organize your content in your Twitter group.

3. **What is a tiny URL?**

   A. A tiny URL is a handy tool for shortening the length of a URL to 25 characters. A shorter URL lets you make better use of your 280 characters. There are a number of sites that offer free URL shrinking.

4. **How do I get more people to follow me on Twitter?**

   A. A good place to start is to follow the top 200 or so tweeps who will follow you back. Add a Twitter button to your website, email, and/or blog. When you start following someone, send then a direct message and thank them. Fridays are known as "Follow Friday" days and a good day to tweet something like this hashtag: #ifollowback and you'll be thrilled with the number of tweeps that will find you.

5. **Is everyone on Twitter real?**

   A. There are people that use robots to make the posts to their account, and there are also people who pretend they are someone else. A common misrepresentation on Twitter can create a security and privacy issue. If you don't know them personally, err on the side of caution and treat them like a true stranger (no matter how friendly they may seem).

6. **Why do people stop following me?**

   A. This isn't always personal. Some of the really big tweeps follow thousands of people and they use bots to get new followers and drop followers. Other reasons why people might stop following you is that you are tweeting just too much, or you are posting content they aren't interested in seeing in their timeline. Don't take it personally! You'll unfollow people for the same reasons. It comes with the territory.

7. **What should I say on my Twitter posts?**

   A. You can talk about whatever you

want but make posts that have value. You can promote your business at the end of each post with a link to your website.

8. **If someone is following you is it rude not to follow them?**

A. Follow who you want. You don't have to follow someone just because they are following you. However, you will get more followers if you do return the favor according to research.

9. **Can I delete a tweet that I've posted?**

A. Yes. On the right side of your message on your profile page, there's a garbage can. Just click it and off to the trash it goes.

10. **Is Twitter addictive?**

A. Yes, be warned, Twitter can be addictive. If you feel you are fighting a Twitter addiction you might want to speak with a cognitive therapist about your online experiences.

18

CREATE THE MOST POWERFUL TWITTER HEADLINES OUT THERE

Nowadays Twitter is the place to share links. When you post good content and it catches the attention of your Twitter followers, it spreads like wildfire. Suddenly you have a great deal of traffic from people who have never even visited your site before. The key is to share quality traffic and create powerful Twitter headlines.

This will help you to build excellent traffic flow.

Bottomline, there's more to Twitter than just the value of your content, it's about whether your content is viewed. Remember, you can have the best value but if nobody is looking or reading it doesn't matter, and that's where the headlines come in.

Have you heard of the 80/20 headline rule? What this means is on average 8 out of 10 people will read the headline, but only 2 out of 10 people will follow through and read the content. Headlines are typically seen in web pages, magazines, and newspapers. These numbers get even worse when it comes to email and RSS readers. There is such a battle for the attention of the reader.

Now think about the number of people on Twitter – all with a limited amount of time available to read content. People scan quickly looking for what seems to be the most interesting and that's what they'll opt to read. So, you can see why the headline is so important.

Your headline is a promise to your follower. It promises that they will be rewarded with something interesting and valuable if they click the link. If you want to make sure your headline is compelling, then use the "4-U" rule taught by top copyrighters and journalists

1. Be "**USEFUL**" to the reader,

2. Provide him with a sense of "**URGENCY**"

3. Convey the idea that the main benefit is somehow "**UNIQUE**"

4. Do all of the above in an "**ULTRA SPECIFIC**" way.

The 280-character limit of Twitter has resulted in some professionals recommending you keep your header short. However, most professionals would agree that rather than focusing on keeping your titles short, **focus on creating the best heading in the least number of words**.

DID YOU KNOW - Here's an interesting stat – 55% of the most effective headlines contain eight words or less.

It's all easier said than done right? Writing a good headline takes practice. Like the lotto, you must play to win! Keep practicing and monitoring the reaction (engagements) to your posts. IF you're interested in improving, you will. Keep working at it.

Now, you're ready to create your own powerful Twitter headlines and to enjoy the benefits of those headlines!

19

RETWEETING

Now let's talk about getting your tweets spread even further and increasing the chance of meeting even more people by using 're-tweets'.

Re-tweeting is a common practice on Twitter where you'll re-post someone else's tweet that you like, and you think your followers will like.

With this method, you take the original Twitter message someone else has posted and rebroadcast that same message to your followers. To do a re-tweet, simply click the retweet button on the Twitter website which will set up the post. You have the option to Retweet and to Quote Retweet. The Quote Retweet is an interesting function because it offers an opportunity for you to create your own unique messaging attached to another user's posts. One thing to consider is analytics. IF you simply Retweet the message, you won't be able to view the analytics associated with the post. If you Quote Retweet (essentially creating a unique message that attaches itself to another's post), you are able to view analytics. If you're into measuring your engagements, ALWAYS quote Retweet.

REASONS TO RE-TWEET

When broadcasting the message, you should definitely give credit to the original poster. I know at first it may sound like this will only be good for the original tweeter, but retweeting can actually benefit you just as much if not more because:

1. **It provides more value to your followers.**
   — When you provide value to your followers, you make them happy!

You are also more likely to attract followers. Providing quality content is always a great way to build your business no matter what platform you use.

2. **It will benefit your brand.**
   — If you point a reader to a source of good information that is truly relevant and beneficial to them, the amount of trust that they have in you will increase.

3. **It will help you build relationships with the original posters.**
   — Retweeting someone else's content is an act of kindness, and for the most part bloggers like to return the favor. You shouldn't expect someone to re-tweet your content just because you retweet theirs. Just keep in mind that your chance of being on the other end of a re-tweet increases as you retweet.

Retweeting is all about providing value to your followers so if you want others to retweet your post then you want to make sure that you are providing them with quality content worth tweeting about.

The bottom line is retweeting is a great way to add quality and value to your Twitter page. If done right, retweeting can help you educate your followers, build your personal brand, increase future traffic, and connect you to other great people in your niche.

Just be careful if you use it incorrectly, retweeting can actually hurt your personal brand and future traffic. You want to treat your followers like gold. Don't ever send them to inappropriate websites or spam them with one sales pitch after another.

20

THE ABSOLUTE WORST TWITTER TACTICS FOR SMALL BUSINESSES

We hear a lot about Twitter tactics for small business, you should also know the worst Twitter tactics for small businesses. While experienced Twitter users may be able to recognize those tactics that would be best left unused, those new to Twitter may not be so lucky. So, let's point out a few of the worst Twitter tactics.

1. **Talking about yourself**
   — If you are sitting beside someone

that can't stop talking about themselves, you know how poorly that goes over. It's no different when someone insists on continuously tweeting about themselves. Your followers know you have sales, they know you have a business to promote, but instead of the same old self "rah-rah", why not tell your followers what makes you and your business different from others?

2. **Using auto direct messages**
   — We see it often – a recommendation to use auto direct messages. While there is a place for DMs they shouldn't be abused. Make sure the one you are using works well otherwise followers will be upset and you could lose them as followers.

3. **Using hard-sell techniques**
   — While selling can be done on Twitter (many do it each day), don't expect to build your business on it. Soft sell techniques work much better than hard sell techniques. Before you can sell something to someone your followers have to trust you. Take the

time to build confidence and trust before you try to sell to your followers and skip the hard-sell techniques.

4. **Boring and with no value postings**

   — It should be no surprise that if your posts are boring or they have no value people are going to get tired of following you. Don't just type to type. Really people don't need to hear from you that bad. For example, don't tweet "it's a great day," or "we had an excellent month of sales." Your followers are busy people and they haven't decided to follow you just to have annoying posts fill your day. So, make your posts have value and your followers will stay.

5. **Handing off your social media activities to an employee who is a novice**

   — It's so tempting. You're the boss, right? Posting on Twitter seems like an administrative duty. Remember, using Twitter effectively means you are incorporating strategy and business goals into the equation. Not saying your administrative staff can't handle it. But let's be honest, unless you have experience with social media, it doesn't matter what your title is, a bad social media manager can really drag down a company. For example, I recall seeing a company's social media Twitter accounts in which their admin managed poorly. Aside from the self-serving likes they manufactured from the company account to their own personal Twitter account, the account was like a bump on a log. It was meaningless for prospective clients to even see the page because it looked like a glorified like fest of one (and only one) employee. That's not going to cut it. Presenting unprofessional social media activity is a quick way to lose current and future customers.

Now you know the five worst Twitter tactics for small business, so when tweeting avoid these tactics and you'll enjoy what Twitter can do for your business.

21

TWITTER SECRETS FOR THE SOCIAL NETWORK CHALLENGED

With all the buzz around Twitter you'd think this site had been around for decades. Twitter isn't just for business, internet market, and the savvy social networkers. There are many individuals who are new to social networking and want to use Twitter but are feeling very intimidated. Great news – here are some Twitter secrets for the social network challenged.

TACTIC #1 – FIND FOLLOWERS

Start by finding some followers. It begins by building Twitter relationships. There are millions of users on Twitter and so it shouldn't be too difficult to find other users who share interests with you. Follow them, and they'll likely follow you.

TACTIC #2 – COMMUNICATE OPENLY

Communicating is another important tactic. The whole concept of Twitter is the ability to communicate over long distances. Once you find someone you want to follow or that's following you, make sure you take the time to keep the lines of communication open. That's how lasting relationships on Twitter are built.

Retweet, retweet, and retweet some more. If you see something you'd like to share with others, don't be afraid to retweet. It's a great way to expand your network of followers and share information that has value.

TACTIC #3 – USE HASHTAGS

Hashtags help you to find interesting tweets. The # symbol is the "hashtag" and it is used to mark specific keywords in a tweet. It allows you to build followers and find people you want to follow.

TACTIC #4 – BE AUTHENTIC

When you are posting you should be authentic. Be yourself – don't put on false errs. Your posts should also be engaging. People hate boring posts, so give them something interesting – maybe a useful tip, something inspirational, a news alert, etc. It doesn't matter as long as the post is genuine and offers real value.

Twitter users grow each day. Many of the new users have no experience in social networking, especially in understanding Twitter. These Twitter tactics are a great place to start. You'll be a pro in no time at all.

22

TWITTER TACTICS FOR B2B MARKETING THAT WORK

Twitter is growing by leaps and bounds. As it grows, Business-to-Business professionals look for the most effective way to use the power of Twitter in the inbound marketing program. A recent survey done by marketing professionals surveyed 722 B2B marketers who professionally used Twitter, found that the B2B companies have the greatest success when

- ✓ they monitor their brand,
- ✓ invite prospects to relevant events, and

✓ use Twitter to drive traffic to their website.

You can learn from those B2B marketing with these useful Twitter tactics that the survey discovered.

1. MONITOR YOUR BRAND

Thanks to the many apps mentioned in this book, it's easy to create search queries for Twitter pertaining to monitoring your brand and even the brands of your competition. It's easy to monitor and use that information in your business.

2. INVITE PROSPECTS TO RELEVANT EVENTS

In person relevant events can be very successful when it comes to B2B marketing. You can forge new relationships and strengthen those relationships. You can show followers your expertise and use that authority to position you in the industry. Sharing valuable and relevant content will also lead to an increase in your following. And remember to think outside of the box. Events can be virtual and provide very effective interactions with prospective clients and customers.

3. DRIVE TRAFFIC TO YOUR SITE

You can pair Twitter with content marketing, whether that's a website, a blog, a newsletter, a podcast, a webinar, or a video. Twitter can help you easily distribute your content and drive traffic directly to your site(s). When you link to your site, use headlines that grab attention, it improves your click through rate. We should mention that direct sales are the least successful tactic. The best tactic is to build relationships, which will then increase the traffic to your site.

The B2B marketing community comes together to share news, product information, and insights. B2B marketing is important to the networking and growth of the business. These Twitter tactics can play an important role in the growth of your network and ultimately your sales growth.

23

THE 30,000 FOOT PERSPECTIVE

5 KEY TWITTER TACTICS THAT CAN HELP YOU

Whether you are using your Twitter account for business or personal, it can be hard to make Twitter work for you. When you first start to use Twitter, it's exciting but at the same time it can be really overwhelming. After a couple of weeks, you want to be seeing the benefit otherwise you'll begin to feel like you are wasting your time. Wouldn't that be a shame? These 5 key Twitter tactics will help you get the most out of Twitter.

1. LISTENING

If you haven't heard, social media is about conversation and that includes listening. Twitter is yet another social media tool. On Twitter listening translates to reading the posts from your followers and replying to them.

2. MONITORING YOUR PRODUCTS

Sure you could run an individual search for your products and/or brands but it would be a lot faster and more effective if you used an application like Twitter Search, which will let you set up a column in Tweet Deck where you can monitor any mention of your products and/or brands. Set up as many searches as you like.

3. FINDING QUALITY FOLLOWERS

There are millions of people on Twitter. You want to find followers that are relevant to you or your business. These are people who are really interested in your tweets, which can lead to some excellent connections with potential clients, new or existing suppliers, and professionals in your industry. Again, you can use Twitter Search to make the process of finding quality followers much more effective and faster, but there's even a better application called *Tweet Spinner*, which is best described as a Twitter CRM.

4. CHECKING YOUR TWITTER INFLUENCE

While you can use *Tweet Spinner* to identify the best people to follow and those to stop following, you will need to review each account to determine whether they are worthwhile to follow. This is an important process. Being hands on with your follow decisions will help you be more connected to the relationship-building aspect of the process.

5. SHORTEN YOUR TWEET LINKS

You have only 280 characters to tweet and that's not many, and really you should only use 240 characters so that there are some characters left for links. There are many tools available that will shorten a link, and many are free. Http://bit.ly is free – all you have to do is register and start to enjoy shorter URLs.

These 5 key Twitter tactics will help you make the most out of Twitter whether personal or business related. Keep these handy and you'll be well on your way to building quality Twitter relationships that will become long-term connections.

24

THE POWER OF THE FOLLOW

Twitter is considered the fastest growing social media site on the planet. In 2008 it had upwards of 3 million users and by 2009 that number had grown to 8 million, and then by march of 2010 it had grown to 14 million. Today, in 2020, Twitter has 330 million users.

The key to building a business network is the quality of your followers. Twitter users can follow one another just like friends follow one another on Facebook. If you choose not to have strangers following you, in Twitter Settings simply set your privacy box to manually approve. But if you close your Twitter account to people you don't know you can't take advantage of the true networking capabilities of Twitter.

Grow your following by adding people to your network. Lady Gaga has the largest following with more than 82 million followers. It's time you learned some of the most powerful Twitter tactics to maximize your Twitter power in case you're not well…. Lady Gaga.

1. You should follow those who follow you. This will give you maximum exposure and help your Twitter network to grow.

2. Let your tweets show your real personality and let them get to know you. For example, perhaps you are a writer; why not share some writing tips.

3. Make your tweets valuable to your network. Keep them on topic and interesting. Let your follows know you are an expert in your field and on the topic.

4. Be sure to retweet the posts of other tweeters. Using an app like *Tweet Deck* can make this seamless, especially if you have a large following.

5. Become familiar with "Follow Friday," which is the time to tweet to your favorite followers. That way others can learn about these followers and they can be added to the network.

6. Finally, perhaps the most important tactic is to learn the tactics that the experts like Rich Bryda use, because if they have built empires using Twitter, you can too by learning the tactics they use.

25

RESEARCH AND SHARE

RESEARCH YOUR TWITTER MARKET

Let's jump right in and talk about how you can use Twitter to conduct your market research. Every business has a target market, but the simple fact is that many business owners often miss the mark because they don't know the true needs of their market.

By using Twitter, you can easily listen to the needs of your prospects, the issues they are currently facing and the kind of help that they want.

Whenever you meet someone new on Twitter it's a good idea to try to establish a good relationship from the start. Think like your customer. You buy from people who you trust and like. Your target market also behaves the same way. It is important, especially in social marketing that you get to know your clients and do your best to win their trust and confidence.

A good rule of thumb is to try and keep 90% of your tweets full of helpful content and try to limit your promotional ones. By doing so, you can attract more followers and hopefully customers.

SHARE YOUR EXPERTISE

In order to show off your expertise on Twitter you will want to post quality content on your blogs, website, and other sites, like Pulse Articles on LinkedIn.com. Then share them with your followers.

As we talked about in the last chapter, there are a wide variety of tools that work with Twitter that will automatically check the blogs you've posted and share them instantly on your page. Offering educational materials, seminars, video training and networking events will also go a long way when you are trying to convert your followers into paying customers.

If you're not camera shy, consider using Periscope (now owned by Twitter) to livestream to your audience. Periscope allows you to stream live video on your Twitter page and chat real time with your followers! This will be a fantastic way to make an instant connection for you and your peeps.

There are so many different techniques that you can use to foster the transition from follower to customer by using Twitter. Just remember to keep the value of your content high and the volume of your promotions low and you will begin to see more of your followers clicking on your promo links and turning into customers.

26

HOW NOT TO BE A TWIT ON TWITTER

As of October 2020, there were more than 330 million registered Twitter users, so it is no surprise that there are a few twits in the bunch. For those of you not familiar with what a "tweeter twit" it is:

A foolish or annoying person on Twitter or a person not worth following on Twitter

So, what are the signs that you are a twit on Twitter? So glad you asked.

1. You follow less than the 10% of the people who are following you.
2. You only tweet to people who have more followers than you have.
3. You have a follower count that is a negative number.
4. You tweet only to the celebrities (you know they'll never tweet back to you)
5. You never bother to reply to your @replies.
6. You seem to find yourself tweeting your follower count many times.
7. You send an auto direct message that says, "check out my blog (or website) with a link.

Great now let's look at how not to be a twit on Twitter:

1. BE YOURSELF – always be real. Let your personality show, even on company posts. After all, you don't want your posts to be boring. When your followers can feel your personality, you'll feel more approachable and that's good for business.

2. DON'T BE ARGUMENTATIVE - not everyone is going to like you and not everyone is going to like your company. Twitter is a platform that is sometimes used to voice annoyances or how they are dissatisfied with a product or service. How you handle these situations says a lot about you and your business.

3. DON'T JUST TALK, LISTEN TOO – a good tweeter listens to what others are saying, asks questions, and shares information when they can be helpful. With Twitter, you can build a strong customer base if you are there for your customers.

4. GO FOR QUALITY NOT QUANTITY WHEN IT COMES TO FOLLOWERS – some people get too focused on the number of people they follow and even use software that automatically follows anyone who follows them. What you should do is choose those you follow based on interests. You can search by keyword to find individuals or businesses you'd be interested in following.

5. POST MEANINGFUL POSTS – don't just post to hear the keys clicking. When you post make it something meaningful, something your followers will be interested in. Otherwise, you could find yourself labeled a twit and they will quickly un-follow you.

There you have it – there's no reason for you to find yourself assigned the nasty label of a twit on Twitter. You have all the help you need to become a well-liked (or better yet, well respected) tweeter with plenty of followers.

27

THE BIG FOUR

4 TWITTER TIPS TO INCREASE TRAFFIC TO YOUR WEBSITE

Savvy businesses have learned how important good traffic is to the success of their online business. Many website owners have become proficient in using Twitter to increase targeted traffic to their website. Here's your chance to learn some Pro Tips.

TIP #1 ALWAYS INCLUDE A LINK WHEN YOU TWEET

When you tweet, you should always include a link to your website, because this will increase traffic to your website. Don't include more than one link in your tweet or there is a high likely hood that it will be treated as spam.

For example, if you are posting a tweet to send followers to an interesting link, don't also add a link to your website. However, if you've posted an informative comment be sure to post a link to your website.

TIP #2 TAKE IT VIRAL – ASK FOR RETWEETS

One of the most powerful aspects of Twitter is the "retweet" capability. Retweet allows you quickly take your message viral. Don't assume your followers will retweet something – ask them! One thing to consider – there are 280 characters in your tweet – use them wisely.

Retweeting is a great way to break free of the immediate circle of your followers and reach out to a much larger audience.

TIP #3 CONTENT IS KEY

Just as the content on your website is key to success, content in your tweets is also key. Keep your tweet short, to the point, and easy to understand. With followers receiving an endless number of tweets a day, they don't have time for long tweets. Only post things that will benefit your reader. <u>Avoid tweets that are personal</u>. Notice the underline here.

Okay, this must be said. IF your Twitter timeline looks like a long-demented soliloquy related to one person in particular, delete your Twitter. There's no nice way to say this, you look immature as an adult using a social media platform to air out personal grievances that you are clearly unable to resolve in real life. Sound harsh? That's how others will view it. Don't pin the snide comments, stop liking a majority rude and crude posts that may say what you're afraid to outright post. It's all bad and no one cares about who you're talking about, because you've distracted your audience with your own negative posts. Let me repeat – <u>avoid tweets that are personal if you want to be perceived as an adult</u>.

TIP #4 UNDERSTAND THE PREFERENCES OF YOUR FOLLOWERS

Take a little time to try to understand what the preferences of your followers are such as any specific interests, and if there are topics they like to read. If you aren't sure – why not just ask. However, usually all it takes is to closely monitor what your readers are posting about, reading, and retweeting.

This can be really beneficial when it comes to better understanding your followers and your website visitors. When your readers are understood you are able to create content that is far more appropriate, thereby increasing your click through rate.

Twitter is an amazing tool for increasing traffic to your website. It takes work. It takes you dropping the personal, individual mentality to develop a business approach to growing with your customers (current and future). Learn to maximize Twitter for your business and you've got a solid strategy in place for your continued success.

28

DON'T ENTERTAIN THEM FOR FREE

One of the greatest tools we have is analytics. Oh, I'm an analytic fanatic! If there is a way to measure it, I will, and I will do it often. I have learned such valuable information about my customers, fans, and yes even biggest trolls just by studying the analytics. When social media first became popular, it entered most of our lives as an entertaining hobby. We were entertained by the posts we read; and we reciprocated with entertaining posts of our own.

People share so many facets of their lives from births, to childhood memories, to hopes and dreams, to even deaths. As the months and years rolled on, platforms like Facebook became the repository for the presentation and representation of our lives. Somehow along the way the idea of trolling leapt from the physical world into the digital world. People could anonymize themselves and become someone else. Even worse, they could multiply the anonymity and present themselves as a legion of people for better or for worse (mogwai to gremlins).

More than 1 Billion people are active on Facebook

More than 100 Million people actively use Instagram each month

---

More than 330 Million people use Twitter each month, 48 million in the US

Enter into the realm of combining marketing concepts with the evolution of trolling. Groups began to form using advanced concepts of SEO with the technological "gifts" of multiplication. Suddenly an opinion could be elevated and integrated into our timelines as if it was the gospel truth. Yes, the great tools of social media began to be used against us even in the simplest ways through what we view on our timelines.

And then people got into the game. Using the data available to us all publicly (physical characteristics, the connection to other people and relationship networks, etc.) to form an opinion about someone else. Stringing together words filled with triviality, that may never be stated directly to the person's face.

Yes, the world jumped into the trolling game full force through social media platforms and under the guise of "free speech". It was destined for things to get out of hand quickly. All of a sudden, social media became weaponized and sub tweeting was a real thing. The irony is that sub communication has always been a "thing". The difference is that now the world could see it, respond, join the band wagon, or form in protest of.

To the troll, the world seemed smaller, and yet

felt bigger. The troll felt as if they were "telling the world", when in fact they only had 40 active followers even if they bought 2500. LOL. That's laughable but seriously, that's what the foundation of most trolls rests on - a small legion of boom that is entertained by troll behaviors.

I periodically take inventory of my own social media posts and ask some very fundamental questions about the root of the posts:

— Why did (or should) this post matter?
— Will this connect to my business goals and objectives?
— Could the world have lived without this post?

I adopted this mentality for one main reason:

I refuse to entertain people with misguided social media posts for free (or at all)

It is so easy to fall into a pattern of posting to show off or show up someone else. Luckily, I can say I've never gone that far. But have I chosen to time posts for the trolls? YES, guilty as charged.

It is human nature to tell people to 'back up' when you feel they've overstepped their bounds with you.

In reality... what does your commentary really do to a troll? <u>It feeds them</u>. Trolls do what they do to get attention, to get a rise out of you. Your response feeds the troll, and they continue. In the end, you've performed for free and probably were entertaining for free. And those business goals and objectives, they either remained stagnant, or you pushed yourself further away from achieving your dreams.

If your goal in life is to shut down the haters, it's time for you to select bigger goals.

Making a hater "shut up" is such a small goal contrived by small-minded thinking.

I look out every single day and I see the promise of a better society with my help, not because of my social media entertainment. I cannot be the person I am while battling

Twitter trolls, there's not enough room in life for both. There's just not enough me to go around. I need you to feel that same way about yourself.

SO, I ASK YOU...
— Why did (or should) this post matter?
— Will this connect to your business goals and objectives?
— Could the world have lived without this post?

Be big enough in your thinking and your mindset to know that you are bigger than the trolls from the beginning. You stooping to respond to a troll makes for entertainment and is probably costly to your own brand.

Keep your goals and dreams in front of you and you'll be so blinded by the achievement of goals, you won't even see the trolling.

History shows us that court jesters entertained because they were showcasing the best of what they had to offer. Allow your goals to be bigger and better than that of a court jester. Bottom-line, don't entertain other people for with your own ignorance. It will be the costliest move you can make online.

151

29

LET'S GET SERIOUS

WHEN PEOPLE WEAPONIZE TWITTER

I've been a social media maven for quite some time. When Twitter first started in 2006, I took immediate notice and a liking to the platform. It was a relatively new concept that was competing with the unlimited character communication of Facebook at the time. Limit words to 140 characters...egad! But we learned. We learned to be efficient with our words and to use the heck out of abbreviations. A unique language carryover from the pager days (...remember the Motorola Timeport?).

Twitter reimagined communication in a new platform that allowed sharing. It was social media open to the public. Whereas Facebook felt personal, designed for a family and friends circle, Twitter opened up the idea that it was a megaphone for the internet. You could say what was on your mind and voila, everyone would know. It is indeed a great tool, always has been. The trouble with tools, is that when we make them accessible, but don't show people how to use it, or bound people with restrictions, bad things can happen.

Fast forward to today. The now 280-character per post social media platform has done a pretty good job of regulating the harm out of the platform through their policies. I love the opening two sentences in their policies:

> *We believe that everyone should have the power to create and share ideas and information instantly, without barriers. In order to protect the experience and safety of people who use Twitter, there are some limitations on the type of content and behavior that we allow.*

There is power in sharing. It is when the sharing

of ideas and information becomes abusive, harassing, and harmful that Twitter rightfully steps in. There's also a little thing called the 1st amendment right in the U.S. (for the U.S. people). There's a fine line and a balancing act that Twitter monitors to insure that

1- they're not infringing on someone's 1st amendment rights
2 - the user is not violating someone else's constitutional rights
3 - the user is not violating the agreed terms and conditions to have an account on the platform.

All three of those criteria help Twitter determine who should stay and who should either get a timeout or a goodbye forever. Sounds dramatic but it is an important feature of the platform. Users must feel safe that they can share ideas and communication without being harmed by another user's attack.

WHAT TWITTER IS NOT

The policies are in place to help the platform and communications move along in a non-threatening, safe way. Twitter is not the police.

Twitter is not your mom. And Twitter most certainly is not someone else's mom. If someone says they don't like you on Twitter, that doesn't violate a Twitter rule. That's an expression of an idea, an opinion. That's fair game. If someone targets you by repeatedly messaging you, tagging you, threatening you, harassing you, etc., that is in Twitter's domain. According to Twitter's policy,

> *Re: abusive behavior*

> *In order to ensure that people feel safe expressing diverse opinions and beliefs, we prohibit behavior that crosses the line into abuse, including behavior that harasses, intimidates, or uses fear to silence another user's voice.*

Twitter rules go on to spell out what they define as hateful conduct and the boundaries of such on their platform:

> *Re: hateful conduct*

> *You may not promote violence against, threaten, or harass other people on the basis of race, ethnicity, national origin, sexual orientation, gender, gender identity,*

religious affiliation, age, disability, or serious disease.

What I love about the policy is that it gives an opportunity for people to report whether they were the target or the bystander. Twitter evaluates and makes a judgment call. Also know that

Twitter is well versed in the "reports" that come through with bad intentions.

I've had the good fortune of chatting with Twitter professionals, and yes, they've heard it all. While the number of false or unsubstantiated reports come in are relatively small, they've seen them, and they don't waste anyone's time on the matter. Once Twitter reviews the complaint(s) and the user account or post(s) being reported, Twitter is really good at getting back quickly and saying why they will or won't take action on the account (pointing to their rules as the basis for the decision). The net to catch the nefarious reporter is in place as well. Don't worry, just because someone may not "like you" won't get your account deleted if they false report your activity. It just doesn't work that way. The

Twitter rules were written by people with sense.

CROSSING THE LINE

Where I find the line becomes blurry is when people like and/or retweet posts that do in fact cross the line. I do not see a policy that protects against the sub tweeters that are too coward to draft the message as an original post, but seemingly all too proud to like and retweet a harmful or abusive post. This should be addressed. Liking and retweeting harmful posts are the same as the original poster. It breathes life into an ugliness that should not be on the platform, and that should have consequences. There is nothing normal, sane, or okay about liking a tweet that wishes death or harm on someone. This is the part of Twitter that has slipped through the cracks and I would recommend an update in the policy to address.

I watch these silly "Twitter beefs" over what I will say sound like the most insignificant topics and ideas. Relationship drama is a prime target for the ugly back and forth. Reading the vicious nature of messages when a person decides to air out their dirty laundry on the platform is eye-popping. And don't let folks start "going live" through Twitter's live streaming feature (Periscope), and the words leap off the page into a full-blown soap opera. Whoa... Is that what people are doing now? Again, I go back to the fundamental way people regarded Twitter - like a megaphone to the world. Is this what you think the world is interested in hearing? And from you?

Twitter cannot and will not be the referee or the mediator for verbal disagreements. Twitter is not there to help you resolve your conflict. I see people get caught up in the drama of asking Twitter to "fix their life" or their problems as if Twitter is Iyanla Vanzant. Twitter is none of those things. Twitter cannot heal a person, it showcases what people choose to post, that's it.

THE RULES FOR CELEBRITIES

It's an interesting observation that celebrities seem to get the brunt of the attacks on social media when it comes from multiple people. When something hits the news, the Twitteran (or tweeple, or tweeties, or whatever is your term) they step into the conversation in full force. It's disheartening to read some of the horrible things people say online through an account that is fairly disconnected to a real identity. Here's a few (warning, these are ugly, and they are very real):

— "I hope you fall off a cliff and die"
— "You are the biggest piece of s..."
— "You can't sing worth a crap and should never open your f.... Mouth again"
— "Why do you even exist as ugly and fat as you are"
— "Your wife and child should be raped 1,000 times for choosing you"

If you believe what you read, people are unimaginably cruel. If you step into the wrong stream, you'll feel sick and dirty by reading the hate and filth that people attempt to spew. The irony is that the comments above came from users who kept their identity anonymous. That's the new dynamic in social media that we're in.

The stones and rocks are being thrown, but we can't pinpoint where they're coming from.

That's a serious problem. Twitter can shut down accounts that break the rules, but what is stopping someone from creating another? It's a scary time we live in that people dedicate so much time to hate. Luckily, Twitter uses more than a name and email address "to catch a social media killer". The IP address and other factors help pinpoint a user who is creating multiple identities to harass and harm.

Even in my own world, I've experienced hateful comments directed toward me in my inbox and on various social media platforms. I use the safety tools to block and report the offenders, and things generally work out. If I find someone a threat, I take action. If I don't think you're a threat, I'll give you all the time, space, and opportunity to either tire out, or do enough that the police or other officials decide to take action. It's that simple. I don't sweat the small stuff. Going back and forth on Twitter (or any other platform) is small.

Small time thinking produces small results.

IT CAN GET SERIOUS QUICKLY
There's the example of Charlotte Dawson in

Sydney, Australia who was hospitalized after a suicide attempt that occurred weeks after being viciously attacked through the platform. Bullying is serious. The comments in her case were astounding. People wished death upon her, excruciating pain, karma, and the like. These people had never even met her!

Why feel that way? She was a judge on America's Next Top Model in Australia when the attacks turned vicious. Perhaps she judged a fan favorite unfairly, who knows. But is it okay to take a reality show that far? To insert yourself into the real life of a woman on a television show? There's a sick mentality that tells a person this is acceptable. This case did not have a happy ending. The ongoing cyber-attacks reportedly exacerbated her battle with depression. In 2014, the America's Next Top Model in Australia judge took her own life at the age of 41.

Cyber bullying and attacks have consequences for the targets, the attackers, and anyone connected (even bystanders). The toxicity of cyber bullying can be so consuming, that it manifests into a terrible tragedy. When these attackers "tweet then delete" their attacks, the damage is done. They may have cleared away the message from view, but the damage was caused, the gun fired, and there is no taking it back. It is so incredibly irresponsible to just say whatever mean thing that hits your brain, and yet people do it without regard to impact and consequences.

A University of Wisconsin study was conducted in 2011 that found on average 15,000 bully-related tweets were sent out daily. Yes daily. How's that for a dose of toxic with your morning coffee? What do you think the number is today? There is a common theme among those users endeavoring to bully online, it's not typically one statement, it becomes a campaign for them; a way of life. The Charlotte Dawson case is a prime example. There were particular trolls who spent a large amount of time gearing their messaging toward her. And again, I will repeat, they had never met her.

ON THE FLIP SIDE

No matter where the number is today, we

know that bullying online is a problem. On the flip side, there are many eyes seeing the messages and people don't say anything. I cannot understand how you rationalize seeing hateful and harmful comments and you look the other way. But isn't that how many people react in society? They look the other way. It becomes so much easier to look the other way when you see someone going off the rails when you can just click away. Sadly, we have increased the number of witnesses seeing the cyber shots but have decreased the number of leaders willing to take a stand against the improper use of the tool. As an online community we have to improve. See something, say something.

USE TWITTER PROPERLY AND IT IS GREAT

I personally see nothing wrong with Twitter. It has connected me to some amazing people in my personal and business life. I love the fact that we are given the megaphone to speak. I also love the fact that Twitter is responsive when you have an issue and resolves problems that they are legally able to resolve. Twitter is not a babysitter. Twitter cannot make someone like you more, talk about you less, etc. Twitter is a social media platform that offers 280-character posts in a micro blog style format. If you don't like what you see, Twitter does have a logout button (that works very well) as well as a delete account button (that works very well).

Be safe out there in the "twitterverse". We have the ability to create good and positive outcomes in social media. It starts with having good intentions, and the rest is growth and relationships.

ABOUT THE AUTHOR

Hello everyone, I am **Jennifer "drJ" Thibeaux** and I would like to THANK YOU for taking the time to read my latest book project,

U Are What U Tweet Dot Com. This book is being released in Fall 2020 as a book in multiple formats – print, online, and audio. A derivative of an earlier version of the content, I felt it was important to relay where we are now with social media and our own communication and relationships with each other.

Like my previous book release – "Positively Charged – Invest in What Makes you Stronger", I accepted the challenge to write amidst some of our darkest hours as a nation and within the world. COVID-19 was not only our greatest challenge, but it pulled back the rug of our greatest shortcomings, fears, and failures as human beings relating and living with each other. Social media has become an electronic megaphone to shout people's feelings about their experiences. Some people are alone through this. Their social media "audience" is truly their family. This pandemic has forced us inside and online like never before and here we flock to a system most don't understand. To be honest, many people get caught up in the matrix. Seeing and saying things they wouldn't dare say face-to-face. Online has made it easier to be ugly, anonymous, and confrontational with little to no consequences. Online also makes it easy to spread positivity, connect, and be heard. It boils down to how you view it and how you use it. I'm hoping this book level sets your ideas and expectations for social media so that you can get ~~something~~, no strike that many positive outcomes from it.

Just a few words about me – I burst onto the public scene as an exceptional gymnast and Olympic hopeful starting at 5 years old in Houston, TX. At an early age I represented brands like Girl Scouts of America and United Way in national print and television ad campaigns. As an exceptional student I graduated in the top 4% of my class at Willowridge High School turning down over 10 scholarship offers from top schools to accept my scholarship to study at Texas A&M University at College Station.

As an adult I've had the pleasure of working all over the globe as a researcher, educator, and consultant; giving international press conferences on my social science research; providing business intelligence and guidance to some of the most influential leaders in America and beyond. I have worked with schools all over the United States and in South Africa to improve youth outcomes of hope, wellbeing, engagement, economic energy, and financial literacy through scientific research and curriculum development.

I am the co-creator of one of the leading mentoring models for attorneys, entrepreneurs, and executives – hosting leadership conferences around the United States to support leadership development. I have become a thought leader in web broadcasting; assisting groups like the National Diversity Council to deliver their nation-changing courses.

 I have served as an activist and voice for African American and Hispanic students at Texas A&M University to defend against systemic racism, harassment, exclusion, and division – holding the position of executive director of the largest minority student organization on campus during my tenure as a student. I am an author multiple times over and have multiple degrees. Additionally, as a long-time philanthropist, I am an Endowed Century Club donor at my alma mater – Texas A&M University. I have also had the pleasure of chronicling the journey of many retired football players as they pursue benefits earned through documentary film projects.

Finally, one of my most important roles has been to be Liz's mom and biggest fan. I call her Liz; the world knows her as Liz Smith #24 on NCAA Division I University of the Pacific Women's Basketball Team #UpRoar

Let's connect on Social Media & Online

Twitter: @JennThibeaux

SoundCloud: @JenniferThibeaux

LinkedIn: www.LinkedIn.com/In/Thibeaux

Company: www.Thibeaux.org

Blog: www.TheDrJBlog.com

Research Firm: www.ThibeauxResearch.com

Technology Firm: www.Kuronix.com

THE READING CONTINUES...

Released 2020. Publisher: Thibeaux Publishing
- Self-Help book that motivates and encourages techniques of positivity in order to improve one's life. Written in the backdrop of the COVID-19 pandemic, this book focuses on manifesting success, despite your circumstances.

Released 2020. Publisher: Thibeaux Publishing
Social Media How To book published to teach mastery of social media marketing and branding in business. In this book we explore the strategies for success to identify your audience through social media; identify strategies that support your overall business goals; build marketing lists for short and long-term sales cycles; the power of content and sharing, scaling up through target marketing, and investment using profits of your marketing results.

Released 2018. Publisher: Thibeaux Publishing

- Self-Help book published to transform the ideas of a Vision Board into practical methods to transform your life
- Based on adult education and learning principles, transformed into a digestible workbook that helps readers pinpoint areas of improvement and make the changes.
- This is a book you can and should take everywhere to keep your vision and goals in your line of sight and within your reach. Goals happen when you prioritize them.

Released 2017. Publisher: Thibeaux Publishing

- Self-Help book addressing one of the world's most pressing but largely unspoken issues - adult bullying (focusing on bullying committed by woman toward women.
- Based on research and a collection of real-life incidents, the book helps victims of bullying identify the signs and regain their strength through the ordeal by using Principles of Sun Tzu.

Released 2017. Publisher: Thibeaux Publishing

- The ultimate "this is how we did it" book. The book covers raising a high potential youth athlete and how to navigate the waters of club and school sports.

- Additionally, the book covers the mechanics of supporting a youth athlete such as capturing editing, and publishing film, social media, and the college recruitment process.

Released 2012. Publisher: Insight Publishing

- Anthology with notable authors – Stephen Covey, Jennifer "drJ" Thibeaux, Dr. Tony Alessandra, and Patricia Fripp

- A collection of authors who have made a trailblazing impact on leadership and success. Jennifer Thibeaux adds her perspective on success in the sports industry.

THE LISTENING CONTINUES…

Available on all major music streaming platforms